The
Gates of
the Elect
Kingdom

Winner

of the

Iowa Poetry

Prize

The Gates of the Elect Kingdom

Poems
by
John
Wood

University of Iowa Press Ψ Iowa City

University of Iowa Press, Iowa City 52242

Printed in the United States of America

Design by Richard Hendel

http://www.uiowa.edu/~uipress

Printed on acid-free paper

Library of Congress Cataloging-in-Publication Data

Wood, John, 1947–

The gates of the elect kingdom: poems / by John Wood.

p.   cm.—(Iowa poetry prize)

ISBN 0-87745-581-3

I. Title.   II. Series.

PS3573.05946G38   1997

811'.54—dc21   96-46332

CIP

01   00   99   98   97   P   5   4   3   2   1

FOR CAROL

no better state than this
οὐ μὲν γὰρ τοῦ γε κρεῖσσον καὶ ἄρειον
ἢ ὅθ’ ὁμοφρονέοντε νοήμασιν οἶκον ἔχητον
ἀνὴρ ἠδὲ γυνή.

Contents

Acknowledgments

Grateful acknowledgment is made to
the editors of *Cultural Vistas*, *Poetry*, and
the *Southern Review*, where some of these
poems first appeared, and especially to the
editor of the *New Orleans Review*, who was
kind enough to publish the title poem in
its entirety.

I

The Gates of the
Elect Kingdom

FOR PAUL GÉRÔME

Bless the man who can restore the spirit.

— *Wilhelm Johannes Hoade*

Proem

I originally considered subtitling *The Gates of the Elect Kingdom* "An Historical Poem" because it is based on historical characters, historical events, and what is certainly one of the great visionary moments, probably the last of such moments in pre-War, mid-nineteenth-century America — the founding of the Hoadeite community in Kansas. In fact, the story of Wilhelm Hoade, his visions, his coming to America, and the establishing of his community is a compact American epic comprising all the best and most hopeful dreams of pre–Civil War America.

In the poem I have tried to be faithful to those characters and events; however, at times I have, of course, manufactured dialogue, minor details, and so forth, but at no point is there anything in the poem that could not have actually happened or that is unfaithful to the history or the teachings of the Hoadeite movement. In fact, many of Hoade's own words — except those in the *Vision* poems — are taken from Hoade's *Mysteries*, and even the *Visions* are influenced by the descriptions Hoade gave of them and that were recorded by his followers after his death. The historical facts of the Hoadeite movement are fairly well-known and even entered the American artistic consciousness in the 1930s and 1940s with Aaron Copland's ballet suite *Seven Hoadeite Dances*, choreographed and danced by Martha Graham, and Rockwell Kent's beautifully illustrated edition of Hoade's sermons, *The Mysteries*, published by the Limited Editions Club.

Wilhelm Johannes Hoade (1788–1852), founder of the Family of the Elect Kingdom, known as the Hoadeites, was born in Germany and emigrated to the United States with his followers in the mid-1840s. They established a vaguely socialistic-messianic agricultural community of about a hundred individuals near Manhattan, Kansas, where they believed Jesus's return would occur in 1857. Hoade died in 1852, but the community continued to flourish until 1858 when the members began deserting it. By the end of 1859 all but Adolphus Winkler, one of Hoade's original "Twelve Elect" in whose name the actual deed to Kingdom Farm passed on Hoade's death, Winkler's wife, Alma, his two daughters, Eva and Clara, and their husbands had departed.

For readers interested in more information, probably the best work on the subject is Paul Kettle's *The Hoadeite Community at Kingdom Farm* (Manhattan: Kansas State University Press, 1958). Nedie Lyon's essay "Hoadeite Hymnody" in the January 1932 *American Choral Journal* is also quite interesting and important because it influenced Copland's ballet and is still probably the best work on the musical life at Kingdom Farm. Occasionally, rare pieces of Hoadeite folk art appear on the market, most notably a beautiful Hoadeite wedding cup consigned to Sotheby's in 1962 (see *Historical Americana*, Sale 1001, May 25, 1962, lot 33, photograph on p. 64), of which only two others are known, one at the Walker Museum at Kansas State University and one at the Wilhelm Hoade House in Manhattan.

My interest in Hoade as a subject for a poem is actually an outgrowth of my scholarly work in early photographic history. I have published several volumes on the daguerreotype, the first photographic process, and almost anyone who has studied the literature of this process has encountered both the name and visage of W. J. Hoade. While the well-known St. Louis daguerreotypist John Fitzgibbon (see my *The Daguerreotype* [Iowa City: University of

Iowa Press, 1989], p. 120 and plate 14.) was in Kansas making his famous series of American Indian portraits, he happened to take a picture of Hoade that has been reproduced many times. Fitzgibbon even left a short record of the sitting in "Daguerreotyping," an article that appeared in the *Western Journal and Civilian* 6 (1851), pp. 200–203, 380–385. He wrote, "After leaving the camp of Kno-Shr, I traveled to the Hoadeite community near Manhattan, having read of Herr Hoade and his Elect Elders in the press, a fact of which I informed him upon our introduction. . . . When I suggested he pose standing, for Hoade was an extremely large man, and holding a Bible, as it is the common manner to pose with the instruments of one's trade, he replied, 'Mr. Fitzgibbon, what you read about me in your papers must surely have been inaccurate. I fear you do not know me at all,' whereupon he placed the beads I had presented him around his neck, took up a sickle, a handful of wheat, crossed his arms, sat down in the posing chair, and said, 'Now, Sir, you see me as I am.'" The power of that portrait and the quirkiness of Hoade's response intrigued me.

Hoade's importance was probably best summed up by F.R. Leavis in his *Scrutiny* essay "Mythic America: Peaceable Kingdoms and Utopian Visions." He wrote, "Compared to Young and the Mormonian Latter-Day Saints of Utah, Hoade's Elect were failures; compared to the Shakers, their craft-work was bizarrely baroque; compared to Robert Owen, Hoade was no true 'reformer'; but considering them all and compared to them all, his *vision*, simple and beatific, was, without doubt, the most visionary."

A Vision of Kansas

And He came unto me saying, *Wilhelm,*
rise up from the abundance of the Rhine
for I will wither down its grape, for I
will scatter out its vine, for I will dream and sow
its furrows dry with fireless flint
that will not strike a wine for Elect lips:
an Elder's scriptured kiss or the plain mouths
of maids. And they shall turn and put their backs
in shunned disgust to all the Rhine and rivers of greed,
and they shall rise and bring their sickles cross a wheat
where lands lay down in gold and prosperings.
In the Christ-farm of a heart's bleak need alone
shall I be found, in the stubborn soil and the wheat's bright grain.
Rise; go.

And Hoade took up his atlas and knew
that God had called him to Kansas.

The Beginning of the Progress

He preached of the new world
and the exodus from the old,
and soon there gathered about him others
for whom the word *Kansas* was also
God-touched, fertile and shimmering,
awaiting their plows. And they sold
all they owned and bought passage.

I have wandered within the compass,
the elect and measured arc
of love's geometry; come hand in hand within
and hand in hand with me.
I've divined joy's pure theorem
to plot the equations of grace,
seen Christ aglow in the eye of the child.
Hand in hand we'll take up the plow
and build His Kingdom's farm on Kansas plains.
And Christ will come to harvest all our yield
Shoulder to shoulder plowing Kansas to Paradise.

The Imminent Return and the Congress of the Elect

And Hoade spoke of the Millennial Congress
and the sacred year lost in Gregorian inaccuracy,
of 1857 and *The Imminent Return*:

Let the women be neglectful of the canning of beans,
their cooking, and all the stuff of kitchens,
but let them be combing with love,
setting the lightning of their high loaved hair into wifely gifts
and dreaming of husbands coming home bigger than Jesus;
let men be driven by the girl-lust
they cannot carve from their sight or cut
from their grip and gait; let girls
weep for rapturous rinks and angel-boys askate and sweating
round an erect and risen Christ; let the world
hunger for their preacher's yeasty breath, his rising hands,
the born-again moment immersed in Christ's ejaculant fire;
let the world convene
and take up their wounds and gather in congress
to announce the protocols of their anger; to issue
the drafts of their secession from centuries
of numbed control, from pyx and chalice
and all the vestments of shame; to indict
the long priesthood of self-castration;
to await the undoing of the past,
the breaking from high clouds of earthly canticles,
to await the slow fall of shuddered glories in bright shafts,
godhood mantling down in ripplings of Kansas light,
to await the Christ-herald of the rapturous hour.

The Injunction .

Know history as you know the soil and the seed, the compass, the square and the beam, Christ's embrace and the hold of your love.
— *Wilhelm Hoade,* The Mysteries, *III, ix, 2*

The man with no patience for history
is frightened of mold.
He constantly brushes the backs of his books
and watches husked corn as it dries in the bin.
He can feel the grit of its spores
as they grind and rise in the sockets of his hips,
or lace along a femur's length.
He smells it on his childrens' breath
and nightly fears he feels its dirt
curving round his wife's great thighs.

The man with no patience for history
longs for a Paradise halted as stone.
He shines his tomorrows bright to their burning
and guards his slipping hours,
but hours cannot slip in Kansas light,
cannot slip from fields of grain,
cannot slip in works of love.
And Paradise was never still.
The past's decay is future's hope.
And in this moment work and wait
and Christ will come and set you free.

Melchior and the Butterflies

It was Melchior who first saw them,
Melchior who first heard them.
In the long hall of beds he lay
with the Elect dreaming of Christ
loading high the haywain,
stacking the abundance of Kingdom Farm,
and baking it into loaves; Jesus calling
for flour and milk, and the great white bowls
of brown eggs stacked so high children marveled,
and the children handing out the bright loaves,
and everywhere the odors of yeast and ovens,
of morning and fresh bread, but then
Melchior's dream turned with the odor of vanilla,
and he awoke, and vanilla was in the air
and everywhere, and up and down the long hall,
and he looked out, and it was as if
all the monarchs of Kansas had come,
as if Kingdom Farm could lift into the air.
And he awoke Hoade and the others
and together they walked in their smocks
through acres of butterflies. And butterflies
lit on their arms and in their hair, and Hoade wept
and understood. And in the evening they lifted,
but Kingdom Farm was drenched
for weeks in the rich dark secrets of vanilla.

Divisions of Labor

I

Sometimes I tire of teaching
and think of the other women,
the ones in the kitchen
or those in the gardens
digging and planting. They get
all the praise — and daily!:
"Why I've never seen such fat cabbages;" or
"This sausage is better than any
I ever ate in München." That kind
of stuff. "Oh, Sister, your potatoes are like — "
angel turds, I thought; Christ, forgive me, but
that is what passed through my mind once
listening to some old Elder going on
to Sister Bertha. All I ever hear
are things like: "But why must we
speak English;" and "Why must we
read music;" or "I don't need geometry
to build a barn." Later they'll be glad —
when their barns don't fall over,
and English and music are natural
as German. But by the time a learned thing
becomes second nature, the teacher is as forgotten
as first nature's long-gone tutor.
None will ever look back to Sister Anna
and beam as they would for a cabbage.
The group's greater good, the Kingdom's abundance, is,

I'm told — and retold, my dutied concern, but when they're all,
all so — so stupid, so stupid and rude,
a greater good is a difficulty to fathom,
harder even than a Paradise to come
on Kansas fields.

II

I must have mixed a whole tablespoon
of horseradish into Anna's portion
of sauerkraut yesterday. Those big
bright eyes of hers went red, the tears
ran, and she downed two glasses of water.
"What is it, Sister? Oh, Anna,
what is it, dear?" "Taste this, Bertha,"
she screamed, and the whole hall was looking on.
"Oh, Sister, I can tell by the smell
that some of the horseradish the other Sisters
were making must have fallen in your portion;
can't you smell it, too?" That was great fun.
She disgusts me with her ways,
her little harp and clarinet and perfect English.
She won't even use German when it's all us
together — talking privately of certain matters.
She with her little classroom all her own
and me in a kitchen shared with ten others,
and my little Hannes coming home and saying things
like, "Nein, Momma, Schwester Anna sagt

es ist pronounced best *doll-ar* not *ta-ler*."
Christ, there's not enough horseradish in Kansas
for her. I know I'm to love us all,
but love is no easy thing. And I seldom feel like Christ
chopping cabbage, stuffing sausage day in day out
and listening to the other women. I wish I had time
to sit down sometimes and just think — about anything,
or listen to my Hannes play his clarinet.

The Expulsion of the Heretics

They are as dangerous as wagons,
those intense, soft voices
clabbered up with flatteries
and what sometimes sounds
like desire. Such tones
could web away a man's
whole heart and drain it down
like a dry gourd on a vine;
yet they can look so sad
in their cast downs, so
St. Sebastianed, erect
with arrows, so St. Agathaed, breasts
laid out, the blind
would weep, the dumb stir
lips into low declamations,
and the long deaf hear again.
Oh, we've held them close
and paid in all the corn and currency,
the wealth of fields and vineyards,
paid in all the abundance the flesh
can negotiate. But now, here in Kansas,
they are gone, and let them stay,
and let us keep our lusts
and know them and be thankful,
but let desire's draining angels be gone,
gone to weave and web another place.
And in their scurried leavings,
see them as they are, see them grown brighter

and more proficient from our embrace, polished now,
bright as a cock's gaff, and glittering,
their red clocks gleaming, sanding down
another's days. And so, they've driven off — fire flung
from their wagons — toward orchards
or fields of berries or snow
or some preferable somewhere,
furious and sulking at how demanding
our wishes and needs, at how unfair
the terrible ordinances of love.

Exultation: Melchior Tobit, the First Black Hoadeite, Leads the Service at Kingdom Farm on New Year's Day 1851

Little Babe Jesus don't let nobody sink
that'll grab the life line. No sir;
he don't let you sink. That little ol' baby hand
just gets ahold like a lover and pulls.
O Lordy how he pulls, that little baby. Why,
he the god of fire; he the shock; he the flambations
of the spirit, the burnations of love; he be love
all bundled up, the outlaw of love; the outlaw of love.
He come up from behind and stobs you
with his pearly knife of love, stobs you
in the ribs, and you feel love movin' then,
movin' like the Pentecost, movin' in your mouth,
in your shirt, in your pants, movin', movin' and you
want to scream and tell everybody about love.
Love makes the cats flex they whiskers
and the great whales leap for joy;
it makes the panthers shine at night
and the white rabbits dance in the light.
Love's the cocoon of fire.
And He the Betsy Ross spinner
of your soul. He the tailor
of your celestial suit.
Ooooh Jesus, take your scissors
and trim me till I be good enough.
O Lordy, dry my throat out

like the fish heads in the sun,
give me the fresh hot pig blood to drink,
give me the meat of castor bean,
the juice of unboiled poke to quench my sin.
Burn up my sin with your love.
Let me see into the lightning center
of your sight; burn out my eyes.
Ooooh Jeeesus, fisher man,
throw out your net and pull me in
and let me be worthy to be caught,
worthy to be set before you to break with bread.
Fix me on your holy spit and
turn me turn me turn me
till I'm worthy. O farmer god,
plow-master and driver,
drive me with the burning love.
Brothers, Sisters, do you feel it?
The god of fire,
the outlaw; the shock. And He love us all.
Makes no difference. He love us all.
Black and white and German and Indian
and cannibal and head hunters too,
and all the children,
all the children of the world.

And Hoade arose and said,
Ah, Melchior, it is so; it is so.

Chivaree and Dance for the Marriage
of Melchior and Carla

They clanged the pots; they clanged the pans;
they broke the dishes and rattled the cans;
they beat on the windows; they beat on the door
to chivaree Carla and Melchior.

But in their bed and deaf to the din,
he held, he touched, he took his bride,
glad for the lust they neither could hide,
glad for the shapes their shapes were in.

Within that dance of lust and gene,
desire's psalm of give and take,
they rose and fell for their bodies' sake,
like no waltz, nor reel, nor buck and wing, like no stepping they
       had seen.

And glad for the Lord of Love's entrancing,
the crowd outside being its dancing
to the strings and flutes and the golden harp,
all swinging and winging till the day twirled to dark.

The Omega Vision

A Christ-storm of fire in a steepled field spinning,
God Himself thundering the rows of frenzied thorn,
His iron sandal's fall for a dance of thinning,
the black bloom of His frown, the graving of the ground.

That is what I told them,
and I did see Him, gigantic, frightening,
tearing through the corn
setting it ablaze as His robes, all pure flame,
touched the stalks. And I watched Him,
and He looked into my eyes.
And His hands
were like birds swooping
and tearing at those fat with sin
as if they were the harvest.
And the fields flamed-out in blood
and the blood drove the flames like whale oil.
And bones were crackling at His fingers' touch
like stormed branches in the wind.
And He said to me,
To make the Kingdom spring
will take the nailed and hammered joy of Jael.
Love me less and the kernel will not crack.

And He turned from me
and the hem of His fiery gown seemed to spin
and He began to spin, and I saw Him

lift and rise over the ruined fields,
saw Him rising, turning
turning into pure tornado.

The Murder of Melchior

Hoade heard them from his study
calling out, saw the torches through his windows,
and he thought, *Has God sent me newly Elect?*
But going out, he saw into their eyes,
saw flung down at his door
what first in the darkness he thought
a smoldering log, till his eyes adjusted
and he smelled the burned meat of man.
"How you like your nigger now?"

Did you send me here for this, O Lord?
Is this the promised fruit of Kansas fields?
I swore no swords if love were shields
but will not bear a thing this hard.

And Hoade was like lightning reaching out
and he grabbed the man who spoke to him
and plunged his fingers through his eyes
and pushed him to the cold ground
and no one moved as Hoade held him there
and with his massive hands
pulled the man's face from his head
and flung it at the sweating, screaming,
still, unmoving mob.

Hoade's Return

*The Rev. W. J. Hoade of the Kingdom Farm community turned himself in to
authorities last Tuesday night in regard to the death of Sean Cook, a baker, of
Manhattan. Local magistrate Eliphalet Putnam released Hoade Wednesday
morning saying there was "just cause," "wrongs done on both sides," and that
"lives of freemen are of equal value before the law."*
— Manhattan Weekly Traveler, *February 8, 1852*

The hogs and hounds of a rotting god
could not drive me from Christ's own land,
and they've eaten my galled rebuke
and tasted Christ's command.
Under His iron sandaled fury
I've broken the breastbone of sin.
And for this, I am blest,
and Melchior is blest. And though torn
for such blessing, we are risen and radiant;
torn in the flaming trial
we have risen from the furnace whole,
weighed but not wanting
in the days that draw the stations of our blessing.
And now the sunflowers rise and sway for us.
I have watched them in the breezes
of evening, watched them swaying,
watched clouds driving over them
and smelled Christ's breath in the wind,
rich as vanilla.

Love and work will reconstitute the soil,
will fertile the ground for Harvest.
And we will heap high the long table with goods,
and He will return to sit with us and eat the corn,
and pork, pure and clean as doves,
and red cabbage cooked purple as a king's raiment.
And He will drink the cool, amber cider of our trees
in new communion.

He has fled from this glebe
and Beastmen now sow the beast seed.
We have looked into their faces,
seen them in the places we passed,
seen them at their trades
and innocence held harlot for gold.
Shame, shame smolders in the air.
We must tear the beast mask from their faces
and uproot the thorns they've sown,
prepare the fields for Christ and the children's coming.

Sisters, Brothers, though I may not be with you at Harvest,
know that I am with Him, joined in the pit of the peach,
in the apple's core, in the onion's most layered chamber,
in the swaying heads of sunflowers, in their dominion
of the fields, and in their risings and upliftings over the children.
I will be with Him then, protecting
and awaiting you, awaiting you
in the sanctification of innocence.

Lament and Doubts

There was one vision, the last, my sisters and brothers,
that I shan't reveal — and cannot understand.
— Wilhelm Hoade, The Mysteries, *Appendix A*

That first night our wagons rolled into Kansas
butterflies descended
like shooting stars to lead us.
And they angeled us on for days, their bliss
and radiance pulling us, proving Christ attended
and blessed our progress.

We knew the soil would be stubborn as doubt
but the wheat's grain bright, that Christ Himself would help plow
the fields till they delivered up loaves
to lesson all the world in love's
arithmetic, and count love's sum as how
the sum of charity was reckoned out.

Did we stumble toward stars gone out
and swear to break a field of stone?
Could Christ allow such a fate
as Melchior's on a route
of angels? Did the road only lead to charred bone
at what I thought the kingdom's gate?

Carla Tobit Tells the Women That He Is Gone

*Hoade suffered a stroke while working in the cornfields and was not found
until late in the evening after he failed to arrive for dinner. Carla Tobit and the
Winklers sat at his bedside and were careful to record everything he said as he
passed in and out of consciousness throughout the night. He died at precisely
6:00 a.m. on the morning June 5, 1852.*
— *Paul Kettle*, The Hoadeite Community at Kingdom Farm

It was the first time I'd heard him speak in German for years.
It was as if he'd forgotten English, forgotten Kansas,
forgotten us all and everything. Brother Adolphus said
it wasn't Hoade but the stroke speaking,
that he'd so long lain outstretched in the sun and corn
his mind had gone. How else could the Harvest
slip from his lips, could the thought of His coming
and the bread we'd bake take flight.
But it had. Even when I spoke to him of Melchior
he didn't remember. He would just call for his mother.
Mutti, Mutti, he must have said a hundred times.
I thought there would be Words,
a final message, something to set down
or for the masons to cut, a testament.
But there was nothing. At the end he said,
Give me a sip of cider. And Sister Alma raised his head,
and he took a sip and said, *The core of the apple is bitter.*
Gibberish, I thought, but took it down.
And then he said, *Oh, it is so rich the room cannot hold it.*
Open the doors; open the doors or the walls will break

with the sweetness. And he breathed in deeply,
and there was nothing more,
and he was gone.

Waiting for Jesus

They waited from New Year's to Year's End
as expectation and disappointment rose to fill each day,
rose like the ripe sweet stench of silage
that hovered over the farm all summer.
Most thought it would be New Year's;
then that it would be Easter; and then, and then,
and on and on till finally at last on the Year's Eve
at midnight's wide eye's twinkling, they knew
in that sparkled turning He would descend
star-like upon the fields with light falling about Him
and night turning morning, and years and time all falling away
as clocks and calendars began again at noon in the year One.
And so they prepared the greatest feast they'd ever set:
pieces of comb were broken from the hive
heavy with honey and big as hands;
pigs were roasted and glazed rosy
with the jam of sweet plums from last canning;
and hot cabbage in wide wooden bowls
was shredded and sweetened and studded with caraway;
and jars of peaches, pickled and smelling of clove
and cinnamon stick, were opened and set out;
and the long table looked as it never had looked.
And the sisters went about their work
asking the questions they'd asked all year:
"What will you say to Him?" "What will you do
if He looks at you?" "What if He touches your hand
when you set His plate before Him?" And they worried,
"Will I be able to say, 'More cabbage, Lord? More pork?

Some cider for Your cup?' " And the men rehearsed their lines,
      as well:
"We've waited a long time, Lord; thank You for coming."
"Do You plan to shift the seasons, turn winter back,
to begin the planting now?" "Do You need a dray, Lord,
or will Your plow furrow through fields at Your touch?"
And "Forgive us our stupid questions, but this is so new, Lord;
we don't know how it is to work with You, or if we even need to
      speak."
But by six in the morning discontent and anger had set in,
the pork was cold and covered with a caul of grease,
the women had fallen asleep round the long table,
and von Tungeln, one of the original twelve,
said he'd had his doubts, that Hoade was false,
and he and his were heading westward. And rage broke out
like a fire in the corn and faces were dark as bruises
and others said they'd go with von Tungeln
or would just go. And they did and the end began,
and all Winkler's words couldn't stop it:
"Even prophets can misfigure,
but the Vision's still true.
Christ's still coming.
Why leave; life's good here."
But Winkler had no voice for prophecy
or magic and could hold few for long —
and finally none but his own, and they worked
what acres they could and still believed,
still waited, still sometimes picked up
the bright, sweet scent of vanilla on the air.

Emma Goldman Thinks of Hoade

I had read The Mysteries *early on, but what was most convincing was that day*
in December of 1909 when I met Alma Winkler, then in her eighties. We spent an
afternoon together over cakes and tea talking of life at Kingdom Farm.
— *Emma Goldman,* My Life

He might have made a revolution —
or something — rise radiant out of Kansas —
absurd as that sounds, but more believable,
I'd think, than the Paradise he expected
to lift, blossom, and sway in the grains' gold acres.
How could so wise a man have come
to such . . . what? not conclusions —
and *visions* is so — cloudy a word
but for the kind you'd expect him to have:
why he'd read Engels as early as Marx had!
and he called on armies to rescue children,
to attack factories and do — God knows what:
flame the wheel till angels, their fire-blades drawn,
can mend the axle's inner core,
whatever all that could have meant —
something about justice, I'd guess, but that's no way
to organize an army. He was more poetry
than insurrection. But the way he netted people to him!
he could have made those shattering states
correct themselves, hold, and shine
had he not been so *touched* — so sprung
by irrelevancies — the idea of a great harvesting god,
an overalled and farming Christ driving

a hundred Hoadeites and all Kansas
back through the barred gate and into Eden —
lunacy, sheer lunacy, of course. But what I'd give
to have sat with him there at the long table
and sipped the Kingdom cider
looking out over the bright and bending fields.

The Last Survivor

Mary Wentzel Woodard, 93, of Chicago spent the first ten years of her life
at Kingdom Farm, Kansas, the socialistic religious community which was
established by reformer William Hoade in 1844 and flourished for over a
decade. She is the last surviving Hoadeite and ...
—from "Kansas Celebrates 80th Anniversary of Statehood," Life, April 5, 1941

She was too old to remember much,
thought she remembered Hoade, the power
of his voice and word, his giving her a pear
once as she sat on her porch — not likely,
and certainly not his preaching; she was
too young — said the Farm
finally went broke after Hoade killed a man:
memory's old plates etched and effaced and etched again
and again — till so crosshatched and shadowed out
details blur into details, days into days
as we'd wish them lived, a life of reasoned words
at all the proper moments uttered. But her childhood did blaze
again and again when she spoke of taste or smell
or the color of what never quite turned Paradise:
the red flare-fall of elm and oak; or new mown fields
bailed and lofted up, seizing whole barns with scents sweeter,
said Hoade, than Hiram's cedared palace and all glittering Tyre;
or the pungent difficulty of the cheese shed,
the slow fall of milk-white brine from linen bags
rank as the warm, heaped tubs of slaughter time,
but cheese white as Momma's aprons every morning,
cheese better than all the food of the rest of her life;

and a fine dust that powdered the blackberries
she gathered for the breakfasts of Elders,
the humming wasps that nested there
and waited her hand through the brambled thorn;
and everything bathed in light;
and on and on until you knew, till you were sure
memory's reels run true, knew you, too, heard
his voice and tasted the pear, knew age drives
memory Heavenward in spite of error
and that it edits, that it corrects the past
into Paradise.

II Homage to
Dafydd ap Gwilym

FOR DAFYDD GWILYM WOOD

charegl nwyf a chariad

Dafydd ap Gwilym, a contemporary of Chaucer and Boccaccio, was born at Bro Gynin, near Aberystwyth, around the year 1320, and he is thought to have died around 1380. He was the greatest Welsh bard of the middle ages. *Homage*, prepared as a gift for my son, is a loose, free, but artistically faithful translation after some of his major poems, arranged so as to suggest, if not his biography exactly, at least his primary concerns and passions.

Homage to Dafydd ap Gwilym

The foam falls in fleeces big as fists
and snowflakes wander North Wales
like swarms of white bees.
I keep inside, can't sleep.
Even girls can't get me out.
Heaven makes us hermits and January is plagued,
as if God Himself had thrown down
the down of heaven's geese
till drifts billow over heather,
sway like swollen bellies, as if God wills
fine flour down and flour-lofted angels
cloaked in frost and quicksilver
lift the planks of heaven's loft
and dust down the thickets
of Wales like April's blossoms,
as if a load of chalk bows down the trees,
as if a coat of tallow, of cold grit had come,
and mail and dragon scales, a leaden coat
whose rude power makes us wait the rains and May,
the glade of the wood, that girl from Breckon.

*

There on the tide, bright
as snow, as salt and the sun,
the moon-white gull fishes.
It is like a lily light on the waves;
or a nun; or paper, white
for writing; or my letter to a girl. So go now.

Find camp and castle, that girl bright
as Arthur's mother, and say these words,
say that she must say *yes*, that Dafydd dies,
gentle Dafydd, unless he has his way.
Neither Taliesin nor burning Merlin,
magical with girls, loved one prettier.
Oh what color! Those copper cheeks,
the loveliest in Christendom. Oh my God!
Tell her to hurry, to be sweet, to agree
or that girl will be the death of me.

*

Modest Morvith of the golden hair,
that lily-browed girl in Enid's shape,
made passion catch and glow to flame
when in bright leaves once around my neck
her white arms went to take me slave
to lips I'd not known. And now by love's knot
I'm bound as by her arms, white as winter,
when face to face, when sin was simple,
she thralled me down in the brown-bright leaves.
But a collar shy and smooth as arms is slavery
I could take. Arms white as lime are gifts
on any neck. And hers seem torques of gold
and blinding spells, bright beauty's famed design.
And I, blond Dafydd, the wine-bred bard, am bolder boy
for having known them there, and without care

and drunk on her — my slim, my strong,
my Morvith of the golden hair.

    *

Under the green hazels this morning
I heard a thrush sing verses bright as visions.
Morvith, my golden girl from Caer, had sent him here
full of song to sing in Nentyrch dingle.
May-flowers and the green wings of the wind
cloaked him like a priest. And everywhere
was all cathedral. And it was, by God, as if
the altar's roof was pure gold. And then
May's child and music's master
in shining language chanting declared
the gospel: a leaf as Host, and sanctus bell
by nightingale. And as this mass was said
and rose above the hedge, they raised to God
their chaliced liveliness and love. And here
in this grove, I was gladdened by song.

    *

Duthgie, brilliant, shining Duthgie
of darkest, smoothest hair, come
lie down with me in Manafan dingle.
No cheap food I'll spread
but no glutton's feast nor reaper's meal,
nor farmer's fare nor lean and Lenten meat
or English meal. Gold girl, I'll serve you

mead and song, a nightingale's cry and thrush's cheer,
a hidden thicket, a birchen bower. And while in leaves we lie,
the trees will lean to shade our joys.
There birds ride branches, and nine fine trees
will round our rest; above is blue,
and below is clover soft as heaven's flour.
There two — or even three — can lie. In the wild
where oat-raised roebuck ride, where blackbirds
are thick and trees are bright and beggars can't find us,
where hawks are nursed and air is sweet and water cool, there
where passion is frequent and heaven's right now,
that's our place, my honey girl. Tonight, tonight,
you ember-eyed, wave-bright beauty. Duthgie, hurry;
we've things to do.

*

Until I saw a mirror, I'd never known
I was not so fine and fair. My God,
yellow cheeks, a nose like a razor. Terrible!
My eager eyes looked like dumb holes,
my hair — a bunch of weeds!
It might have been a trick, a magic mirror
made of lies, but that would make the world
more strange than even I had thought.
Yet if it's true I might as well be dead
for all my looks are likely to get me.
Goddamn mirror! Dark, blue, moon-glowing
and brightening like charm-work.

It works mortals the way magnets work metal.
Witch-made mirror, swift changing dream,
cold traitor and brother to the frost, go rot in hell!
But if I *am* as haggard as all that, it's the fault
of those girls from Gwynedd. Damn those Gwynedd girls,
so beautiful, so unobliging, so skilled
at spoiling the fine features of a boy.

                *

God damn the girls of this parish!
I'm so horny I'm bent double.
I haven't even had a hag, much less
a wife or virgin in I don't know how long. What's with 'em!
What harm would it do some brown-browed girl
to lead me to the woods and lie down
in shadowed leaves? I'm always in love
and no curse clings worse. Daily I see girls
I'd die for but am no nearer getting
than if they hated me. On Sundays
I go churching but twist from God
to face the fine-faced girls of Llandbadarn.
"Look at the good-looking boy,"
one beauty whispers, "he might be fun."
"Forget it," says the bitch with her,
"that's Dafydd, a real creep,
a gawker. And take a look at that nose."
No more dazed looks for her! I might even become a hermit now,
but I couldn't help turning, couldn't help

staring at such shining. I've learned my stern lesson,
I, strong song's stout friend: I'll bow my head
and go out alone — at least today, at least from this room.

    *

Yesterday I waited out the rain
under a green birch, stood in the wet
waiting on a girl because I'm a damn fool,
but Gwen's face could also launch ships
and make grown men eager as boys.
But it slipped quick as I could sign the cross
when some shaded thing loomed up saying,
Be silent, Dafydd; I,
always naked beside you, am your shadow-self
come to show you — dare you look — your self.
Myself! You? You look like a scarecrow!
Did some jealous husband pay you for this?
You're nothing of me. Look,
I'm young; I'm blond; look at these looks,
you hag-shanked ghost-herder;
bog heron; muck smeared humpback
with a saint-face and lusty look.
Take care, Dafydd; I shadow you everywhere,
lie down with your trysts and shade your lies,
know enough to ruin you well enough.
Well, then let the devil shit you, shade.
I've killed no dogs, no hens with hurling-stones,
scared no children, given no girls

cause for complaint. *But what if I said you had,*
why there'd be whole villages of rage,
and then: a missing poet. "Dafydd, you say?
No I haven't seen him for days"; "Dafydd, oh yes,
last month"; "Dafydd, yes, I think I remember him,
a poet, wasn't he?" Then sew up your lips
to what faults I have, shadow-self. You need me
more than I you, old creep. And though I may lie
to lie with Gwen, you, too, will rise and fall and rise again.

     *

When food and frolic's the thing we're after,
a Welshman's got the longest nose. So,
though the town was new, I quickly found
a lively inn and called for wine. And then
I saw her! Oh God! So slender, so rare;
so rare and slender I ordered roast
and old wine and called her to my bench.
She was shy, but not for long with such a feast
and the stuff I whispered. She said *sure*
and I said *soon as everyone's asleep.*
And then I just thought about her eyes,
dark as her hair and soon to be mine.
Naturally it got screwed up. I bumped the beds,
fell, bruised my leg, hit my shin on a stool,
then ran scared into a table, knocked off a bowl,
got the dogs abarking, and to top it off
stumbled into three crummy Englishmen

in one stinking bed, peddlers: Hicken, Shenkin, and Shack,
or some such names. And one of those scum-mouthed bastards
started yelling, "A Welshman's creeping about;
hold tight to your purses." That got everybody up,
and I, Dafydd, poet, lover, with headache and shin-ache
had to crouch around trembling like a thief.
But I prayed, and thanks to Jesus and all the saints
got back to bed hoping God forgives
the sins we suffer for slim and slender girls.

*

That glorious girl who holds her court
in the grove would never guess
what I'd confessed to the mouse-gray friar.
I went to say my sin: that I was a poet
and idolatrous at that, for there's a girl!
Ah, dark browed and bright faced, a girl
I worship, I want, I haven't had,
my murderer, whose praise I've carried
and loveliness lyricked the whole of Wales,
without success. I want her in bed
between me and the wall. And so the friar said,
"Don't waste yourself in lust
for a paper-pale and foam-white face;
think of Judgment Day, think
of your soul. And quit the verse;
God didn't die for you to write poetry!
And that stuff you write! Fol de rol and rot;

stirs up the kids, gives them ideas.
Dafydd, you could damn down your soul
with such sensual rhyme." But I told him,
"God's not as mean as you'd have Him be.
He wouldn't damn a boy for loving gently,
since women are what the world loves best,
are heaven's fairest flowers — next to God, of course.
Every joy is heaven made, and misery's hell's domain.
You've got to preach; I've got to write.
And I've as much a right to sing for bread
as you to beg those loaves. Your hymns and psalms
are also poems, Friar. Not with one food alone God feeds
the world. There's time to pray and preach,
make song and sing, as well. Poems are sung at feasts
to please the girls, and prayers are saved for church
to gain a different grace. Good friar,
when men are as ready to hear *paters*
as they are to hear harpers,
and Gwynedd girls beg my wanton lays,
I swear to pray for nights and days.
But till that day, there's shame on me
if I sing any hymns but poetry."

III Love's
Lexicon

FOR FRANK GRANGER

unafraid of the heart's bond or the sums of love

For My Father

I'd wheel him strapped to his chair
down the long ramps and out
into the shade of the catalpas
so we could watch them fire the bees,
drive them from the walls of the house
where yearly they'd hive and honey.
And soon a smoke of kerosene
and burnt sugar would drift up
to the trees with the rising swarm.
And the peeled-back boards would reveal
deserted webs, matted and thick as dreams,
and broken bits of comb,
the wild black honey oozing.

I still sometimes dream of him,
of open windows and the long, warm springs,
the smell of grass and wild onion,
the noise of mowers at dusk
and the sway of the great snowball bushes
blooming up and down the length of Second Street,
iron fences and terraced yards
and jonquils that seemed to race April
just to frame our lawn,
and my father beside me,
erect and unbound.

Thinking of My Mother

She lived into her death
and was gone before her dying.
All but her breath
wrecked years before.
Her brain's once lively pages
crumpled into tight wads,
grew hard as rock. Voice, eyes,
teeth, bladder, bowels —
all wrecked in the frail bag
of flesh that once contained
generosity beyond measure.

I am glad, though, it was she
who so long lay there not dying
instead of me. Each visit
broke tears or rage, then finally
nothing from me, nothing
but the desire to flee as I stood there
bending over her, talking
of weather and mail and relatives
as if her ears had not shut
and I had not tumbled from her memory,
as if I would not have rather been
anywhere else.

Had she watched over such ruin
of a thing once me, her only child,
her whole history
would have slipped into disaster,
every breath into regret.

I know this, having my son
here beside me, having learned
love's lessons in her generous abundance.

Remembering a Young Poet I'd Known in College

His going seemed less sad
than that there was so little to mourn
after he'd gone. It was all too artificial
for serious tears — or to matter;
deaths like those don't,
not in the run of things.
He was all parody, myth-mad and anxious to nova,
to flame out young, to beat Berryman by thirty years
and then edge out the whole singing suicide team.
So he blew holes in his chest.
And he and all possibility evaporated, burned off
like morning fog, to mingle
with the fates of other lonesome children:
the fat boy who locked himself in the refrigerator
when his parents said no more cake;
the girl who jammed scissors in her unkissed breasts
because her TV idol liked to get drunk
and drive fast, could now never answer her letters
or desire; and child after fragile child.
So he, too, made his graceless gestures,
large center-stage struts with great waving
of the arms and profiling of the head,
him playing Jack Oakie playing Mussolini,
but to an empty house
and years too soon, years before some grace
might have mantled down to laurel or foil
or merely dignify a tired and tawdry plot
that never worked.

There was no tragedy left, not at that point,
not even the waste; it had set in long before,
back when the good old boys
dead-ended him with praise and he was made to think
he could pick and choose the mask desire would wear.
But I do remember a summer night though
when I could have wept for him,
when we listened to Puccini
over and over till dawn
and drank mavrodaphne, warm and sweet
as his breath,
and he held me,
held me with all the secrets
he would soon have
under his perfect control.

The History of the Kiss

The lips long to complete
the temptations of the eye.
The unravelings of arousal
lie there, and are
the eye's rousings.
They make bread of girls
and bread of boys.

We'd eat the very paint of *Spring*,
break teeth on Apollo's loins
were guards not there
to marshall all our lusts
and hold us back.

And so we lie together quietly
in the futility of language,
trying to shape a logic
to our presences, those conjunctions
of desire and need, those
pilgrimages of the lips,
progresses whereby we learn
the lexicon of our love,
whereby we solve
the syllogisms of the heart.

And this
is the history
of the kiss.

How Little Lillian Found the Lord and Served Him

FOR JOHN METOYER

Yet bitter felt it still to die deserted.
—*William Cowper*

When Big Lillian saw how the spoiled corn
aborted her pigs, she got in her wagon
and went down to the drugstore
and bought her some ergot to feed Little Lillian
who couldn't leave the boys alone.
"I just can't help myself, Momma,"
Little Lillian would say. "Don't Jesus do no good?"
Big Lillian would say, and Little Lillian would reply,
"No, ma'am, He don't." Mr. Verdue, the druggist,
understanding a request for ergot,
also suggested cottonwood. He said,
"Big Lillian, I usually always sell my ergot
with a little cottonwood, and some take
a touch of quinine powder too."
Big Lillian wanted it all,
but when he handed her the package,
she said, "Calvin, this ain't enough."
And so she got her enough
to burn Little Lillian's womb out,
which she did, but not before
Little Lillian had herself an ergot-idiot.
He had kinky hair and was brown as a potato, which pleased
Big Lillian because she could blame it on
Amalene, Old Eva's daughter, "just a terrible colored gal,"
who, she said, had just come back

to Pine Bluff from New York City to leave it
on Old Eva's doorstep and then go back
to her "musician" friend — played a clarinet — in New York City.
Since Big Lillian was a Christian woman
who knew Christian duty, white or colored,
and since Old Eva was far too old to care for any ergot-idiot,
she took it on. And Old Eva,
who was real happy with her new wagon,
never said a thing. Little Lillian took to praying now
and a year later got herself married to a Baptist preacher.
After he hanged himself because he couldn't get her pregnant,
she took to preaching too, acknowledged her ergot-idiot,
and paid five dollars to have his name changed legal
to Lilliansin. Then she and her little brown idiot
started traveling the gospel circuit.
He was five now and slobbered real bad.
She'd pull him up on the stage and say,
"See what I done. If Jesus can wash that away,
which He in His mercy has done, then He can wash away
what you done too. Jesus Hisself made this little colored idiot
as a sign of the times. Repent ye whores and harlots
lest He drive you from His temple. Hallelujah!"
Lilliansin had a little banjo he'd strum wildly
every time she said *Hallelujah!*
And all those awaiting revival, the full taste of guilt's gall,
would stir at his banjo's twangs, stir from mutterings and dance
into the full vocabulary of seizure and ecstasy,
and Little Lillian grew rich and richer

and settled down and built herself a tabernacle
and married a God-fearing man she'd saved
in a truckstop on the outskirts of Albuquerque.
But along the way she lost her little idiot,
no longer preached about him. In fact,
everybody seemed to forget about him
after she said he went off to dentist school.
And Little Lillian and the man she met at the truckstop
started the Christian Radio Club
and in five years had saved enough souls
to open CRC Bible College right next to her tabernacle.
And Little Lillian was president for years,
president so long she forgot who Jesus was,
thought He might have been a little potato-colored idiot,
so long the college had to change its name to CTVC Bible
    College,
so long her toenails turned inward,
and her bowels stopped and she seemed to grow
smaller and smaller until she was hardly there,
hardly as big as a pea or a splinter
from the Cross, so small and lost
in the blue waves of her blankets, lost,
drifting, and as castaway as her sin.

Four Sexual Miniatures

1. Elegant Old Pederast

His cigarettes exuded sandalwood;
the case, of course, was Fabergé.
When he lisped and when he kissed, he would,
when he could, insert *un peu de français.*

2. Mr. Lawrence, Priest of Love

He thought he'd written love's catechism,
but his catechizing only shows us
he chewed the meat of fanaticism
while fingering the rectum of Venus.

3. Romance Novelist

The valley of her breasts and their hot tops
heave, quiver, and glisten like chicken fat
when she starts to lecture her pretty fops
on her art, her struggle, her this and that.

4. Afternoon with an Aesthete

He lizard'd his glass of Cliquot,
sliced himself large chunks of truffled paté,
blew his nose and asked why Giotto
never approached the genius of Boucher.

Transcendental Sex Sonnet

Kantian transcendentalism minimizes the importance of sense experience. Noumenon, the ding-an-sich, *the thing-in-itself, is an object of purely intellectual intuition, as opposed to phenomenon, an object of sensuous perception. In* Song of Myself *Whitman wrote, "All truth waits in all things. . . . the unseen is proved by the seen." Though the alchemical Philosophers' Stone transmuted base metals into gold, the term has come to refer to the mystical substance that serves as the catalyst in the redemption of the individual or anything capable of effecting regeneration, spiritual or otherwise.*

Kant held the purest thought in mind alone
And knew the noumenal was all unseen.
He thought the *ding-an-sich* was like a dream
Which would not bend to love's phenomenon.
Yet poets since the Greeks have always known
That flesh can kindle spirit to a flame,
That it can transform unseen into seen,
Known love alone's that transcendental Stone.

His lips were fresh, were warm as just baked bread
While hers were cinnamon and wild honey.
And when their arms around each other sped,
Their spirits leapt to flame and they to bed
To learn that sweet, that certain alchemy
To be redeemed through *love's* philosophy.

Professional Dreams

FOR DENISE BETHEL

1.

As formless as the tissues
they seek, the dreams of oncologists
spread into their sleep, swarm
and swirl in the dark. A firm hand
reaches out to them
but turns before it meets theirs
to the texture of lung or brain,
bruised, purpled, transforming
to shapes as large as a child or car.
And it takes their hand, their arm
like things from the late shows.
But they are dumb and lack
their little knives or the agile mind
of Vincent Price, and soon
it is all over them.

2.

She dreams of pencils and steno pads,
of her legs crossed in a short skirt,
the pencil going back and forth
from pad to her lips as Mr. Bigboss
dictates the perfect orders of her life.
In her dreams the movies never lied,
never told her that steno pads

and dictaphones were no more
or that tapes and computers were as close
as she would ever come to Mr. Bigboss,
who will never look into her eyes
at a certain point, on an ordinary word,
like *sincerely*, for example, and it would be like
stars oblivious to physics, caste, and fortune,
breaking from their galaxies
and rushing toward each other,
their planets and responsibilities
hurtling outward toward oblivion,
and joy joy joy everywhere in her life.

3.

They are all girls and sixteen summers grown
and all naked, their nipples out
like the erasers on their No. 2's,
their textbooks, legs, minds all open
and waiting for the most wonderful lecture
of their sixteen years. And he begins,
though he cannot remember what he said,
but formulas flow from him. His hands
are like lightning as they chalk
the equations of wonder to the blackboard,
and the girls know they witness miracle.
Though they are still taking notes,
their desks have somehow vanished

and he can see that their legs
have opened wider and their pencils are furious
in the transcription of wonder
and he knows that they will be thankful,
appreciative, for the rest of their lives,
that they will never forget him
or the beautiful algebra of his dreams.

4.

In all his years he has never
spoken like this before.
His voice is deeper, more
like flowing gold than voice,
the quavers like rainbows, wide
as his arms outstretched embrace
as scripture falls from his lips
like perfect pearls before jewelers.
And it is miracle. And they all hear.
Their sins fall away; their lives
change as they turn their backs
on whores and cards, tobacco, beer,
and the words that drive God mad.
And he sees the walls of his church
fall away and their clothes fall away
and they are naked but without shame
and trees are filled with fruit
and monkeys are asleep in the arms of lions.

And the deepest voice he has ever heard
says to him "Thank you; you *have* done well."

5.

She is after him, and he knows it.
The blue light spins over the top
and the siren cries *I'm going to catch you.*
Her partner is no longer with her
but she needs no one as her car turns
into the alley and she sees him,
the serial rapist of little girls,
the beast they'd sought for years.
He is up against the bricks
with nowhere to go, crouched and crying,
begging for the mercy he lacked.
And she is out of her car, advancing.
And oh how he cries when he sees
high in her hand a razor blade
big as a manila envelope.
And she advances, advances
with sure and surgical precision.

6.

The lepidopterist is where
no lepidopterist has ever been.
It is a lost valley, probably in Tibet,

and it is all aflutter
with great green lunas
and marsh satyrs, phaetons
bigger than nets, and Basilarchia
bluer than any waking blue;
Lycaena and Kricogonia
but iridescent as opal;
Neonympha, Epidemia,
Heliconius, and Polygonia
big and soft
as cats and unafraid
and purring like cats
when they are petted.
They all love being petted
having never before encountered
a lepidopterist or a hand.
And all are to be named
for nothing like them has been seen.
And the perfect poem of nomenclature
goes on and on till morning breaks
to spoil the dreamer's pure adamic joy.

The Bathers

FOR JUSTIN CALDWELL

the heart is out of plumb

What drives the eyes, drives them back
again and again? Is it merely so much flesh
and revelation, the nakedness alone?
No, not even theirs, innocent and easy as it is,
though that alone could compel the coolest eye,
compel it to a honed distraction — or to linger.
Attraction? — yes, but that's always inexplicable
and roused effortlessly, it seems, lifts
like miracles
in uncontrolled mystery from face
to certain face and is not particular to them;
nor even desire — oh, there is desire, of course,
but not just for limbs and lips,
those curves of compulsion, their costly lines,
but for the scene itself, for it to be
and be and be, for all those clear years
before the century's turn, for wide light
and water, the ease of them together,
their agile geometry
and the consolation of a settled world,
summer days and shimmering pools
where innocence itself once bathed
in embracing lengths of providing light.

i. *Seurat,* Une Baignade

I was on the other bank
and couldn't hear him,
but I think he was saying,
"Come over here."
I waved back at him.
He could see it was too far,
at least for me to swim,
and we didn't have a boat.
Mama wouldn't have let me
anyway. She'd just opened
our picnic basket and taken out
a roasted chicken and fat spears
of cool, white asparagus.
And he could see she'd put a cloth
on the grass and Papa was waiting.
Maybe he was a better swimmer than I
and he and his brother would swim over later.
I could see that my sister noticed his brother,
was watching me, was also hoping.
After lunch Papa would fall asleep
and Mama would sit and watch boats,
watch the way light jeweled the water,
and the boy and I would play sailboats.
My sister and his brother would stroll.
She was always strolling with boys.
I once told her she would stroll her life away

if she wasn't careful. But she told me
I was stupid and childish, that her days
were made for strolling, that even summer
would stroll away and leave you
if you didn't go with it.

ii. Bazille, Scène d'Eté

I stood there against the tree waiting
for him to turn toward me,
but the two boys wrestling on the grass
were his eyes' only concern.
Perhaps they'd tire in the bright heat,
and he'd tire of watching, would turn
and talk to me, and we'd bicycle back
together, and I'd invite him to my room
and we'd have some wine and pears,
would talk of teachers or books or maybe girls
and the villages we came from,
our mothers' kitchens
and how they smelled in the mornings
and the abundant smell of evening —
Papa's tobacco and hay still stuck to his shoes
and sweat woven into his shirt like a design —
and we'd talk till morning
or till we fell asleep
together to dream of each other,
dream of swimming,

all summer long swimming
silently, slowly, together,
soundless, gliding
deftly as dolphins
through perpetual pools
of shimmering summer.

iii. Cézanne, Baigneurs

We'd been on maneuvers and were camped down the road.
It was Marc and Gilles who first found it.
They came back wet and laughing,
and someone said let's all go
and off we headed, Gilles leading.
He was like things you saw in the Louvre,
things dug out of Italian volcanoes
and that old Popes kept in their bedrooms —
but he was more than looks —
generous and kind and all that. But Marc!
Who knew what Gilles saw in him!
Marc had a girl back in his village,
kept her picture, showed everyone.
He'd return to her some day. Even Gilles
must have known that. But who knows
what anyone sees in anyone; the heart
is an odd clock, I always say.
I told him Marc was no good,
would hurt him worse than any girl, but he just smiled

and told me what good friends we were. Like that day.
That day! That pond! Heaven!
I've remembered it for years.
We were like children again —
swimming, laughing — but what I most remember
is how he just stood there, holding a towel,
looking off, maybe at the trees or the sky,
and he was beautiful. But that wasn't what I was thinking;
I wasn't envying Marc. He was beautiful, but it was more
than that. He looked — I know this sounds foolish —
blessed, like a Bible story —
like something about King David maybe,
but not one I remembered, like some picture
of one that might have been — a figure
on one of those parable cards the nuns used to give us
for right answers — or when we were good —
or knew the things to say.

But this is all gone today.
The last innocence fell away
in the trenches. The last Jonathan,
bright as some forgotten parable
and wooing our perplexed desire,
said good-bye somewhere in Belgium.
The ponds of perpetual summer dried up,
or were blasted.
And love has turned so commonplace
that couples now

need no strolls to rouse their blood.
We've solved the heart's arithmetic
but learned to fear its mythic sums:
the magic lies, the bonding hold.

And so, those crackled boys and peeling girls
look out at our poor luck,
stretch out their hands to ours.
And though we will not touch
or ever be so free again,
we can recall their generous gestures
and turn from the fluxions of stars
and chromosomes, blind, denying
our bitter solutions, denying
our hungering, bestial hearts.

IV Revelations

FOR ROBERT OLEN BUTLER

who has carved the fluid folds

Angelic Revelation

1.

My angel is my fortune — and the mystic made real.
No old beard stalking heaven with sticks
of crackling lightning in his hands,
storming at pig meat, menstruation, and buggery,
appeased by burnt lamb, by foreskins heaped into high piles;
no seductive boy, skin like cinnamon,
muscular as a carpenter and capable of magic;
nor any bliss nor terror they promise
haunt my habits and days.

Yet I do know angelic orders guard, know
they *alone* are *all* that choir and chorus us
through the dark between the stars.

2.

They wing down in scents to hold and stagger us
from dangers common senses cannot sense —
to let us know that fathers passed from flesh
have not passed from us.

They descend in dreams, the winged mares
of warning, and fall as revelation
before the closed eyes of sleep
descending to advise and keep.

Or they come
gowned in glories, wide bolts of light,
full-fleshed and guiding, navigating
the stellar night.

3.

Within the body the angel unfolds
to hover naked and radiant
there in heaven's profane parameters
erect in the compass of flesh,
glowing beyond the degrees of gold or shame or inlaid pearl,
unfolds to reveal heaven, too, is real,
self-given as grace and self-ordained,
unfolds to sing salvations out in rose and pear and cinnamon,
in cautions called from sleep and visions given shape,
unfolds for us to see the heart-star revealed,
the heart's light swell, the dark dispelled.

Gifts

τὰ μεγάλα δῶρα τῆς Τύχης ἔχει φόβον

They do not befall us without price,
the great gifts: the five-foot check
delivered as the cameras roll —
and roll on into our lives until
everything is spent; the easy buttons,
the easy kisses and easy thighs of girls
whose veins have not yet risen
to the bumpy maps of their futures —
and their quick, their easy dependencies
hard as lawyers' teeth;
the big house, the big car, the big boat —
bigger debts, bigger dents, bigger leaks.

Unfortunately, such stuff of dream and fear
does too often descend
to tingle our monotonous days
into pure expectancy. Debt and apathy
are relieved, desire inflamed,
and all our assorted greeds are blent
to the brown nausea of hope.

Even revelation sometimes falls
with such a swiftness
and leaves us cleansed, brightened,
gowned in light, or so it seems,
till we come back or till our graceful fitting

turns perpetual and our eyes shut
to dirt, stain, spittle, crust,
and all the other leavings of ecstasy.

And so I try to pray
for nothing, try wanting nothing
but the simple gifts that fall —
the sight of goslings
the size of my fist diving,
diving for the bread falling
from the hands of my son.

Sacred Celebrations for the Moon's Beginning: Five Menarcheal Songs with Epigraphs from St. Simeon

1. Akathist for the Virgin

*Light. Glory. Come, true light. Come light eternal. Light.
Shining forth.*

At the moon's beginning
she beheld in herself
the out-breaking of light,
beheld galaxies of love
spinning there
where she cradled
her future and pain
and held generations
of unborn need
in the longing
her body had made,
in thorn, in nail,
in the world's blest
but bitter salvage
risen now, spangling
from the virginal moon
and her immaculate
and hunting heart.

2. The Demon Brought down on Breton Fields: Gauguin's Vision after the Sermon Redefined

Phos. Glory. Come reality beyond all words. Light. Shining forth.

St. Michael wrestles down the demon
and Breton fields incarnadine.
The demon neck is bent
beneath a hand of hammered rage;
the demon spine reports
above the gold wings' beat.

And Breton girls as they begin to bleed
will see this scene repair, repeat.

St. Michael wrestles their desire
on apple-bright and sermoned days,
but only women see
and only women hear
their broken demon's cry,
their broken demon's tear.

3. The Cheerleaders at St. Agatha's Middle School

Phos. Dhoxa. Come hidden mystery. Light. Shining forth.

Their days seem to whisper "Hurry, hurry;
you haven't much time."
But soon enough age slithers in
to force the rest of all their days
into the muscled hold of sex and death.

The boys stare where they hope
real breasts wait, even if not for them.
They watch the bells and tassels sway
at the tops of little boots,
and they cheer as they are led to cheer
when the girls leap
and spread their small legs in the air.
They cheer and cheer
for the sight of underwear,
the nylon veil,
the mystery's shield.

And soon on other nights
it's pulled away,
and their bodies thrill
and their voices rapture,
but nothing is explained;
no clouds unfold; no words unlock.
And no one knows anything, anything more
than they did before.

4. Communion at Glendalough

Phos. Dhoxa. Come light that knows no evening.
Phos. Shining forth.

She stood in front
of the waterfall
and posed herself
for the camera
the way her parents
had composed her
for Christ
and Christ's sake.
Her hands pressed
the lace of her dress
and straightened
a crooked St. Kevin
upon her chest
awaiting her
and her confessions'
budding wishes,
St. Kevin waiting
the last candle
she will burn
bright as new blood
this night
before sleep comes
brightly as all
the things

she will not know
that she has wished
and dreamed.

5. *Akathist for Love: The Canonization of Cupid*

Phos. Dhoxa. Come rejoicing without end. Phos. Epiphania.

The honeyed arm of Cupid held
his bow and steadied for the bees
alighted there, but they were stilled
and would not sting. When rising girls
awake to glow in Love's pure fire,
they coax and beg their sainted boy,
O bless the bees of man's desire,
distill the nectar of my joy.

Withdrawal and Return

FOR CAROL, AT YULE

Everything we now see as beauty was for the Celts religion. . . . This . . . brought about . . . the relentless attacks of saints and missionaries on those beliefs and practices of the past they could not incorporate into Christian ritual. Thus in the fifth century St Martin of Tours ordered that a much revered pine tree should be cut down. . . . those who held to the old ways . . . lamented the coming of this new religion that practiced such sacrilege.
—*William Anderson in* Green Man:
   The Archetype of Our Oneness with the Earth

When Martin felled the pine,
the modern world began to sing.
Christ wintered in
and fields went brown.
The grail of gall began to rise.

Bitter clouds blocked and held
and broke the light.
Stones that had for centuries
clocked the seasons' turn
shadowed down in fractured time.
Apples would not fall,
and larks forgot their flight.
Rainbows crumbled in the air.
The oracles of groves and fields
fell back to seed and went to sleep.

But now the church has lost its will
and history's veil is pulled back —

the heaps of bone revealed.
Times have turned,
and fields are fluent once again.
Eloquent in ancient tongues,
they turn and bend the corn,
bend it back to oracle,
to the syntax of seasons,
the gestures of leaves,
the four voices of Her voice.

And now the clouds unlock.
The prayer of corn begins to stir the earth.
And larks and hymns uplift
to ready forth the land.
Seeds long locked in anger break.
The holy pine begins to rise.
And everything is rising now,
rising green and waiting.

The Honey of Hellas

FOR RAÚL PESCHIERA

In the gymnasts' grove thrives the shape
that shaped Athenian mastery,
not the self-sown, self-begotten olive
or the disciplined stone
but the living form made known
in gold proportions
beauty's cartographers alone
might compass out from flesh
to chart in pure geometry:
the buttock's chiseled curve,
the torso's even fall,
and love's enigma held
in gold and Doric balance.

*

And they were brought to their knees
the way no archaic form
had delivered them down,
driven like nothing the most Athenian hand
ever called from stone could drive,
for there in its presence
joy was juvenescent
as the figures of artifice.

And at those measures,
at their eyes' scansion
of the forms' pure promise,
they heard the high harmonies
of Pythagorean song.

*

Apollo and Dionysus,
hold me in your laureled groves
and let their precincts blend:
catch me
in the eunuch-pure
and marbled mathematics
of discipline,
in thought
freed from flesh and fragility,
in logic's harmonious oracle;
bind me in love out-spangling
time and the glittering isles,
out-spangling Delos and Naxos
and the honey-skinned gymnasts vaulting,
glistening there
where also drums and burns
the wine-raptured heart,
frenzied and driven
by no reason reason might devise.

And hold them, too,
in attic grace and attitude,
before their sweet arithmetic
begins to break
and buckle under age's weight,
and love and language
all begin to fail
and no more yield
the choral turn,
the kouros smile,
or youth's dumb honey.

ἡ ποιητική

I dream of perfect forms,
Of poems like Parthenons,
A frieze of fluid words
So cut in Attic odes
    Clarity blazes out to shine,
    And beauty — even in ruin.

Bare marble's windy frame
And gold Athene's ghost
Are all that now remain
To prove, or haunt, the loss
    Of intellect's purest moment
    And beauty's unadorned intent.

Those broken stones sing out
Brighter than any art
My pen or thought might craft
And make me try to carve
    The stone to find that shimmered sound,
    Those fluid folds of her marble gown.

The Iowa Poetry Prize Winners

1987

Elton Glaser, *Tropical Depressions*

Michael Pettit, *Cardinal Points*

1988

Bill Knott, *Outremer*

Mary Ruefle, *The Adamant*

1989

Conrad Hilberry, *Sorting the Smoke*

Terese Svoboda, *Laughing Africa*

1993

Tom Andrews,
The Hemophiliac's Motorcycle

Michael Heffernan, *Love's Answer*

John Wood, *In Primary Light*

1994

James McKean, *Tree of Heaven*

Bin Ramke, *Massacre of the Innocents*

Ed Roberson, *Voices Cast Out to Talk Us In*

1995

Ralph Burns, *Swamp Candles*

Maureen Seaton, *Furious Cooking*

1996

Pamela Alexander, *Inland*

Gary Gildner, *The Bunker in the Parsley Fields*

John Wood, *The Gates of the Elect Kingdom*

The Edwin Ford Piper Poetry Award Winners

1990

Philip Dacey,
Night Shift at the Crucifix Factory

Lynda Hull, *Star Ledger*

1991

Greg Pape, *Sunflower Facing the Sun*

Walter Pavlich,
Running near the End of the World

1992

Lola Haskins, *Hunger*

Katherine Soniat, *A Shared Life*